The Sacred Grail Codes

The Lost Teachings of Christ Consciousness & Divine Mastery:

The Grail Prophecy

Copyright

© 2025 Cecilia Lindhe / Ascended Healing.

All Rights Reserved.

All content within this book, including text, teachings, meditations, mantras, chants, energy practices, suggested diets, and cleansing methods, is the intellectual property of Cecilia Lindhe and Ascended Healing.

No part of this publication may be copied, reproduced, stored, or transmitted in any form or by any means—electronic, mechanical, photocopying, recording, or otherwise—without prior written permission from the author.

Exceptions include brief excerpts for review or educational purposes, provided proper credit is given. Unauthorized use of this material in whole or in part for commercial purposes, redistribution, or modification without consent is strictly prohibited.

For permission requests, contact: **support@ascendedhealing.org**

Disclaimer

This book, its teachings, and all associated practices—including but not limited to meditations, mantras, chants, energy work, suggested diets, and cleansing methods—are intended for informational and spiritual growth purposes only. The author, Cecilia Lindhe, and Ascended Healing make no claims to diagnose, cure, treat, or prevent any physical, mental, or emotional conditions.

Not a Substitute for Medical or Psychological Advice

The information in this book is not intended to replace professional medical, psychological, or nutritional advice. Always consult with a licensed healthcare provider before making any changes to your diet, lifestyle, or mental health practices, especially if you have pre-existing conditions or concerns. If you experience any adverse effects from suggested practices, discontinue them immediately and seek professional guidance.

Personal Responsibility & Spiritual Discernment

Each reader is responsible for their own choices and experiences. The teachings shared are based on spiritual wisdom, channeling, ancient traditions, and personal insights, and they should be approached with personal discernment. Results may vary, and individual experiences will differ. The author is not liable for any outcomes, interpretations, or consequences arising from the application of these teachings.

Energetic & Spiritual Practices

The Christ Light Activations, energy work, and spiritual transmissions described in this book are intended for personal transformation and awakening. While these practices can be deeply powerful, they require inner commitment and self-awareness. Engage with them at your own pace and discretion.

Religious & Historical Context

This book includes interpretations of ancient teachings, historical texts, and suppressed wisdom, including the teachings of Jesus Christ, Mary Magdalene, and the Essenes. While every effort has been made to present these teachings with integrity, they are offered as a spiritual perspective rather than historical fact. Readers are encouraged to explore and research further to form their own understanding.

Ethical Use & Integrity

This book and its teachings are intended to uplift, awaken, and heal. Any misuse of the information provided—whether for personal gain, manipulation, or the distortion of divine truth—goes against the essence of Christ Consciousness. Readers are encouraged to approach this material with an open heart, pure intentions, and respect for the sacred wisdom shared.

Inner Guidance & Deep Spiritual Reflection

While the knowledge presented here is offered as a tool for awakening, true transformation comes from within. The greatest wisdom resides in your own heart and connection to the Divine. Use this book as a guide, but always listen to your own soul's truth and divine intuition.

Legal Limitation of Liability

By engaging with the material in this book, you acknowledge that Cecilia Lindhe and Ascended Healing are not responsible for any personal, physical, emotional, spiritual, or financial consequences arising from the use or misinterpretation of this content. Any practices undertaken are done at the reader's own risk.

For further inquiries, please visit: www.ascendedhealing.org

Table of Content

Copyright	3
Disclaimer	5
The Sacred Grail Codes The Lost Teachings of Christ Consciousness & Divine Mastery	9
What Are the Christ Codes?	13
Opening Transmission: Sacred Grail Awakening	19
Chapter 1: The Corruption of Christ's Message – How the 13 Bloodlines Hijacked Christianity	23
Chapter 2: The Vatican's Hidden Archives – What They Don't Want You to Know	29
Chapter 3: The Suppression of Mary Magdalene & The Divine Feminine	35
Chapter 4: The War Over Christ Consciousness – The Battle for the Sacred Grail Codes	41
Chapter 5: The Final Grail Suppression – How Christ Light Was Buried	47
Chapter 6: The Return of the Feminine Christ – Mary Magdalene's Prophecy & Rising	53
Chapter 7: The Grail Prophecy is Now – Why You Are Awakening in This Lifetime	59
Chapter 8: Anchoring the Grail Light Into the World – Becoming a Grail Keeper	65
Chapter 9: The Path of Divine Embodiment – How to Activate the Grail Light in Your Daily Life	71
The Grail Awakening Initiation	79
Closing Transmission: The Flame Has Been Reignited	81
The Christ Initiation: A Journey of Sacred Remembrance	85
Thank You Letter	87
About Me	89
Glossary of Sacred Grail Terms	91

The Sacred Grail Codes
The Lost Teachings of Christ Consciousness & Divine Mastery

There is a light that has never gone out.
A code hidden in your blood, in your bones, in the very breath you take.
It has traveled with you through lifetimes—through Lemuria, Atlantis, Egypt, and beyond.
It is the Christ Light. The Grail Light.
And it is calling you home.

This series is not a collection of ideas.
It is a living codex.
A multidimensional remembrance encoded with divine frequencies, sacred truths, and powerful activations to awaken the Christ within.

You are not here by chance.
You are here because your soul remembers.
The Grail is not a myth. It is your divine inheritance.
And the time has come to restore it.

Welcome to the Sacred Grail Codes.
Your journey begins now.

"There is a prophecy written in starlight and sealed in your soul—

a memory of the time before forgetting,

when the Light walked the Earth in flesh and flame.

You were there then.

And you are here now…

to remember."

What Are the Christ Codes?

"Christ is not a man. Christ is not a religion. Christ is a frequency.
Christ is the original blueprint of divine human potential.
It is the living memory of God within you — a blueprint buried in your bones, waiting to rise."

Before we dive deeper into the sacred grail mysteries, it's important to understand what we mean when we speak of the **Christ Codes**.

These are not religious ideas.
They are not bound to any church, dogma, or institution.
The **Christ Codes** are the original **Source template** of humanity before distortion—encoded in your DNA, waiting to be reactivated.

They represent:

- Divine union within the self

- Unshakable love rooted in truth

- Sovereignty and sacred leadership

- Service without ego

- Compassion without bypassing

- The embodied merging of Spirit and form

They live within every soul, across all cultures and lineages, though they've been hidden beneath layers of trauma, illusion, and manipulation.

To walk the path of the Christ Codes is not to follow a religion.
It is to **embody divine truth, love, and integrity** in every part of your life.

It is a **return to your divine design.**

The Christ Grid & Earth's Sacred Sites

"The Earth remembers.
Her mountains, rivers, and temples still sing the Christ codes—awaiting your return to awaken them once more.
The Earth is not just land—it is a living library of cosmic memory."

Just as the Christ Codes are stored in your DNA, they are also stored in the **Earth's body**.

There exists a crystalline **Christ Grid** that connects key points of the planet, where higher frequencies of divine consciousness are anchored. These sacred sites are **gateways of remembrance**, and many of us are drawn to them because they hold pieces of our soul's memory.

Key Grail Points Around the Earth:

- **Lemurian Gates** – Hawai'i, New Zealand, Fiji, Mount Shasta
- **Atlantean Remnants** – Azores, Egypt, Mediterranean coastline
- **Kemet (Egypt)** – Temples of Isis, Karnak, and the Nile
- **Avalon** – Glastonbury, UK (The Heart Chakra of the Earth)
- **Lake Titicaca** – Portal between the Divine Feminine and Masculine
- **Uluru, Australia** – Solar Plexus of the Earth, Lemurian Stargate
- **Chartres Cathedral (France)** – Magdalene Grail Lineage Codex
- **Ethiopia** – Keeper of the Ark and lost teachings

Many lightworkers, priestesses, and awakened souls find themselves inexplicably drawn to these places. Why?

Because these lands **remember you**.

You may have walked there before as a temple keeper, an initiate, or a guardian of the codes. The Earth itself is helping you to awaken.

When you connect to these points—physically or spiritually—you are reconnecting to the **Planetary Grail Codes** and helping to **reactivate the Christ Grid for all humanity.**

False Light & The Hijacking of Spiritual Awakening

"Not all light is pure. Not all that shines is truth.
Discernment is the sword of the awakened Christed soul—cutting through illusion to reveal the Light within.

In today's world of mass awakening, many are being drawn into spiritual teachings that *appear* to be light-filled—but in truth, **mimic** Christ Consciousness without embodying it.

This is what we call the **False Light Matrix**.

These are subtle, seductive distortions that:

- Promote spiritual bypassing over true healing
- Worship external ascended masters without inner union
- Teach "love and light" while ignoring injustice, trauma, or energetic parasites
- Channel disembodied beings that **offer knowledge** but rob your sovereignty
- Encourage passivity, avoidance, or dependence instead of Christed leadership

True Christ Consciousness always:

- Leads you back into your own divine embodiment
- Activates clarity, truth, and grounded spiritual power
- Honors both shadow and light
- Breaks illusions, not just soothes them
- Anchors in the body, not just the mind or ether

Discernment is love in action.
You are not here to fear the false—but to recognize it and rise beyond it.

The Return of the Christed Man

"The true masculine walks not ahead of the Grail, but beside her, in eternal devotion.
The true masculine is not the oppressor of the Grail.
He is not here to conquer, but to remember.
He is its protector."

The Grail path is not just for women. It is for **all beings** who carry the divine spark.

For too long, the masculine has been either:

- In distorted dominance (control, suppression, power-over)
- Or spiritually shamed, silenced, and left behind

But now, the **Christed Masculine** is returning.

He is the one who:

- Serves and protects the sacred without seeking ownership
- Leads through integrity, not ego
- Honors the Feminine as an equal, not as a threat
- Walks as King, not as tyrant
- Heals his inner boy and awakens his spiritual fire

Men on the Grail path are being called to:

- Embody emotional mastery
- Reclaim sacred sexuality
- Honor their voice, vision, and power without distortion
- Be the stable pillar for the feminine to rise

The Christed Man is the **sacred counterpart** to the Magdalene Priestess.
He holds the Grail Flame beside her—not above her.

Together, they **restore Divine Union** in the world.

Christed Embodiment in Daily Life – Real-World Examples

"To live the Christ Light is not to escape the world, but to sanctify it—breath by breath, choice by choice."

In Relationships

- You speak truth with love, even when it's uncomfortable
- You practice deep presence instead of projecting old patterns
- You honor divine union through sacred communication and conscious intimacy

In Parenting

- You raise your children with awareness, not fear
- You model embodied leadership and emotional maturity
- You see your children as souls, not possessions

In Business

- You serve from soul, not strategy alone
- Your work is aligned with your integrity and sacred values
- You create offerings that uplift others, not manipulate them

In Healing

- You understand that healing is not about fixing—it's about remembering
- You walk your talk and embody what you teach
- You trust divine timing, not spiritual urgency

In the Mundane

- You infuse prayer into your meals, your routines, your work
- You walk barefoot on the earth and feel the Christ Light pulse through your body
- You remember that every moment is sacred when you are fully present

Opening Transmission: Sacred Grail Awakening

Direct Christ Transmission & Activation

"Beloved one, you have come. I have waited for you."

"Before time was measured, before the world was veiled in shadows, you knew this path. You walked in the light of divine mastery, carrying the codes of creation within your very being. But the world fell into slumber, and with it, the remembrance of who you are, of what you carry, and why you came."

"The time of forgetting is over. The veils are lifting. And now, beloved soul, you stand at the threshold of the greatest awakening mankind has ever known. The Sacred Grail, hidden from the world but never lost, begins to stir within you once more."

"You were never meant to be powerless. You were never meant to serve a world that seeks to keep you blind. The kingdom of God is not in temples built by men, nor in books rewritten to serve the rulers of this world. It is within you. It has always been within you. The Sacred Grail is not a relic, not a myth—it is the divine light of Christ Consciousness encoded within your very essence. It is the living blueprint of divine mastery, waiting to be unlocked once more."

The Activation: Reawakening the Grail Codes

Breathe deeply now, and place your hands upon your heart. Feel the pulse beneath your fingers. That is the rhythm of eternity, the song of the Christ Light that has never been extinguished, though the world tried to bury it beneath falsehoods.

With each breath, feel the Grail Codes reawakening within you. They are not outside of you, nor in the hands of those who claim to hold the keys to your salvation. They are in you, written in the divine language of light upon your soul.

Let the seals placed upon your remembrance dissolve now. Let every lie that has kept you small, afraid, and asleep melt away like mist in the morning sun. The Christ Light is flowing back into your cells, your mind, your soul.
You are remembering. You are reclaiming. You are rising.

No longer will you seek outside yourself for truth that has always lived within. No longer will you bow to systems designed to keep you from your divine inheritance. The time of awakening is here, and you are among those called to restore what was lost.

As you turn these pages, you are not just reading; you are receiving. You are activating. You are stepping into a transmission that will change you forever
If you allow it, this will be your initiation, your remembrance, your return.

"Are you ready to remember? Are you ready to reclaim what has always been yours?
Then step forward, beloved one. The Grail awaits."

Sacred Grail Breath Activation & Christ Light Visualization

The Sacred Grail Activation: Awaken the Christ Codes Within

Preparation:

- Find a quiet space where you will not be disturbed.
- Sit comfortably, spine straight, hands resting over your heart.
- Close your eyes and take a deep breath in through your nose, slowly exhaling through your mouth.
- Allow your body to relax, your mind to quiet, and your heart to open.

Step 1: The Breath of Divine Awakening

Begin by taking a deep breath in, slowly and fully, allowing your lungs to expand. Hold the breath for a moment at the top, and as you exhale, imagine releasing all fear, doubt, and falsehoods that have kept you from remembering your divine truth.

With each inhale, you draw in divine remembrance. With each exhale, you release the illusions of separation.

Breathe deeply again.

- Inhale for **4 counts**, hold for **4 counts**, exhale for **6 counts** (longer exhale releases more resistance).
- As you do this, **imagine golden light filling your body**, gently awakening the Sacred Grail Codes within your DNA.
- Repeat this cycle for **seven breaths**, feeling your energy expanding with each one.

Step 2: The Golden Christ Light Activation

Now, in your mind's eye, see a brilliant golden light descending from above, like a radiant stream of liquid gold pouring down from the heavens.

This is the light of Christ Consciousness, the living Grail energy, the divine inheritance that was never truly lost—only waiting to be reclaimed.

- **Feel this golden light entering the crown of your head,** filling every cell of your being.
- As it flows down into your heart, feel it activating a **sacred, ancient symbol within you**—perhaps a chalice, a sun, a golden cross of pure light.
- Let the light expand from your heart, radiating outward, dissolving all veils of forgetfulness.

You are awakening, beloved one. The Grail within you is coming alive once more.

Step 3: The Sacred Words of Activation

(Whisper or silently speak these words as you continue breathing in the Christ Light.)

I am the living temple of Christ Light.
The Grail Codes awaken within me now.
I reclaim the divine mastery that has always been mine.
I am ready to remember. I am ready to rise.

Feel the **energy shift within you**. This is not imagination—this is real. You are reactivating what was always there.

Step 4: The Final Seal – The Grail's Awakening

- Place your hands in **prayer position** before your heart.
- Bow your head slightly and take a final deep breath, sealing this activation into your body, mind, and soul.
- When you are ready, **slowly open your eyes, carrying this awakened energy with you.**

It is done. The Grail Codes have begun to awaken. From this moment forward, you will begin to see, feel, and remember the truth that was always within you.

Chapter 1: The Corruption of Christ's Message – How the 13 Bloodlines Hijacked Christianity

"The greatest deception was not the denial of Christ's existence—but the distortion of His truth."

For centuries, humanity has been fed a **false version of Christ's message**—one designed not to **awaken souls** but to **enslave them**. The true teachings of Jesus were not about control, blind faith, or obedience to religious institutions. They were about **sovereignty, divine activation, and the direct realization of God within**.

But these teachings threatened those in power. The rulers of the world—the **13 Bloodlines**, the **Jesuit Order**, and the **Illuminati**—could not allow people to awaken to their own divinity. If humanity realized that **God was within them**, they would never again submit to **kings, priests, or empires**.

So, the truth was hidden. Christ's teachings were distorted. And a **false system of control was put in place**—one that still governs the world today.

The 13 Bloodlines – The Hidden Rulers of the World

At the highest levels of global power, a **network of elite families** controls politics, finance, religion, and media. These families trace their lineage back thousands of years—far beyond modern governments or even organized religion. They claim **divine right to rule**, believing themselves to be the true heirs of **the ancient bloodlines of kings, pharaohs, and god-kings**.

These **13 Bloodlines** have **manipulated history**, shaping wars, economies, and belief systems. They are the ones who **rewrote Christianity**, ensuring that the true power of Christ's message would never be known to the masses.

The 13 Illuminati Bloodlines:

1. The Astor Bloodline
2. The Bundy Bloodline
3. The Collins Bloodline
4. The DuPont Bloodline
5. The Freeman Bloodline
6. The Kennedy Bloodline
7. The Li Bloodline (Chinese elite)
8. The Onassis Bloodline
9. The Reynolds Bloodline
10. The Rockefeller Bloodline

11. The Rothschild Bloodline
12. The Russell Bloodline
13. The Van Duyn Bloodline

These families have held **hidden power** over the world for generations. They control **central banks, multinational corporations, secret societies, and religious institutions.**

Their greatest deception? **They infiltrated Christianity itself, turning it into a tool of control rather than liberation.**

The Vatican's Hidden Control System – The Three Popes & The Jesuit Order

Most people believe the Pope in Rome is the highest religious authority. But this is **not** the full truth.

At the top of the Vatican's power structure are **three popes**, each playing a different role in the global control system:

1. The White Pope – The Public Face

- The Pope that the world sees—the one who appears in media, speaks of peace, and maintains the illusion of spiritual authority.
- He is the **religious front** of the system, maintaining the deception that the Catholic Church is about salvation, when in reality, it is a **spiritual control mechanism.**

2. The Black Pope – The Jesuit General (The Hidden Power)

- The Superior General of the Jesuit Order—known as the Black Pope—is the true master of deception.
- The Jesuits are the **military arm of the Vatican**, controlling secret societies, intelligence agencies, and global policies behind the scenes.
- Every world power—from governments to banks—has been infiltrated by the **Jesuits**, who are loyal only to their secret agenda.

3. The Grey Pope – The Shadow Elite

- Almost no one knows about the **Grey Pope**, yet he is the most powerful of all.
- He represents **the hidden bloodline rulers** who control both the White and Black Popes.
- His identity is rarely revealed, as he operates in **absolute secrecy,** influencing global events without public awareness.

Together, these three figures control **spiritual, military, and financial systems**, ensuring that **humanity remains enslaved to false beliefs, false power structures, and a false version of Christ's message.**

The Illuminati & The Corruption of Christ's Teachings

The **Illuminati**, founded by Adam Weishaupt in 1776, was not just a secret society—it was a **continuation of the 13 Bloodlines' ancient agenda**. Their mission was to:

- **Infiltrate religious institutions** and twist divine truth into doctrine and dogma.
- **Control education and media** to prevent people from accessing real knowledge.
- **Replace true spirituality with materialism**, so people would seek power, money, and approval rather than divine truth.

The Illuminati understood that the biggest threat to their rule was **an awakened population that knew their own divinity**.

So they hijacked Christianity, turning it into:

- A system of **guilt and fear** instead of divine love and empowerment.
- A belief in **external authority** instead of inner sovereignty.
- A focus on **suffering and obedience** rather than enlightenment and ascension.

They erased Mary Magdalene's role, removed the mystical teachings of Christ, and replaced them with institutionalized control.

How Christ's True Message Was Distorted

Jesus did not come to establish a **church hierarchy**—he came to show humanity that **God is within them**. His true teachings were about:

- **The Kingdom of Heaven Within** – The divine is not found in buildings or priests, but within the soul of every being.
- **Spiritual Sovereignty** – You do not need an intermediary to reach God; you are already connected.
- Divine Healing & Energy Mastery – Christ taught how to harness divine energy to heal and transform reality.
- **The Sacred Union of Masculine & Feminine** – Balance, not control, is the path to enlightenment.

Yet, the **bloodline elites** could not allow this message to spread.

- They created the Roman Catholic Church, which became the most powerful religious empire in history.
- They burned the **Gnostic Gospels**, which contained the hidden truths of Christ's teachings.
- They **demonized mysticism and energy work**, labeling it as "witchcraft" to prevent people from reclaiming their divine power.

Breaking the Chains: The Awakening of Christ Consciousness

We are now living in the **time of revelation**—the **veil is lifting**, and humanity is beginning to see the deception for what it is.

- People are questioning false religious structures.
- Ancient texts, like the Gospel of Mary Magdalene and the Dead Sea Scrolls, are being rediscovered.
- The true teachings of Christ are re-emerging—not through institutions, but through individual awakening.

This is the **Second Coming of Christ Consciousness**—not a physical return of Jesus, but a **global awakening of divine remembrance**.

The bloodline elites can no longer hide the truth. *The power of Christ* **is not in a church, a book, or a priest**—*it is in YOU.*

And once you awaken, you can never be controlled again.

Reflection Journal

The Corruption of Christ's Message

- What beliefs about Christ or religion am I ready to release?
- How has false spiritual authority shaped my relationship with God?
- What would it mean to reclaim Christ *within* me?

My reflections:

_____
_____
_____
_____
_____
_____
_____
_____
_____
_____
_____
_____
_____
_____
_____
_____
_____
_____
_____
_____
_____
_____
_____
_____

Chapter 2: The Vatican's Hidden Archives – What They Don't Want You to Know

"The truth was never destroyed—only hidden. Those who seek with a pure heart shall find it buried beneath gold, stone, and silence."

Beneath the grand cathedrals and golden halls of the **Vatican lies a hidden world**—one filled with **ancient texts, forbidden knowledge, and the lost teachings of Christ**. For centuries, the Church has carefully guarded these secrets, ensuring that humanity never discovers the **full truth** about Christ Consciousness, the divine power within, and the **true nature of reality**.

Why? Because an **awakened humanity is uncontrollable.** If people knew their true spiritual potential, **they would no longer bow to religious or political rulers.**

The **Vatican Archives** contain some of the most **powerful suppressed knowledge on Earth**—including lost gospels, advanced esoteric knowledge, and evidence of **extraterrestrial influence** in human history. In this chapter, we uncover what the Church has hidden for centuries and why it fears the truth being revealed.

What's Inside the Vatican's Secret Archives?

The **Vatican Apostolic Archive** (formerly called the **Secret Archives**) is a vast underground repository holding over **53 miles of bookshelves**—millions of documents spanning over **1,200 years** of suppressed history.

While the Vatican claims these archives contain only "normal" historical records, the truth is far darker. The **restricted areas** hold **forbidden knowledge**, including:

1. The Lost Gospels & Forbidden Christian Texts

When the **Roman Catholic Church** formed under Emperor Constantine, only a handful of texts were **chosen for the Bible**. The rest were either **destroyed, hidden, or declared heretical**. Many of these lost gospels **contradict the Church's teachings**, revealing:

- **Jesus' deeper mystical teachings** about divine consciousness and energy mastery.
- Mary Magdalene's **role as a spiritual teacher and Christ's true partner**.
- **The secret esoteric knowledge** Jesus taught only to his closest disciples.
- Gospels that suggest Jesus was **trained in the Essene and Egyptian mystery schools.**

Among the suppressed texts are:

- **The Gospel of Mary Magdalene** – Reveals how she was the disciple Jesus trusted most and understood his teachings better than the men.
- **The Gospel of Thomas** – Contains Jesus' direct sayings, teaching that "The Kingdom of God is within you."
- **The Gospel of Philip** – Implies that Jesus and Mary Magdalene were deeply connected, possibly even married.
- **The Dead Sea Scrolls** – Ancient Essene texts that align with Jesus' true spiritual path, contradicting Church doctrine.

Why were these texts suppressed? Because they prove that **Jesus never intended to create a religious empire**—*he came to awaken divine truth within each soul.*

2. Ancient Records of Christ Consciousness & Energy Healing

Buried within the Vatican Archives are **ancient texts on divine energy work**, revealing:

- How Christ **performed miracles using divine frequencies.**
- How the **human body is a temple for higher consciousness.**
- How the Essenes and early Gnostics used **energy healing, sound, and light to transform reality.**

The Vatican **erased these teachings** and replaced them with **rituals that require priestly intermediaries**—ensuring that divine power remains controlled.

But now, these lost techniques are **returning to the world**, as more people rediscover the power of:

- **Light Healing** – Using sacred energy to heal the body and activate the spirit.
- **Breathwork & Fasting** – As the Essenes practiced to cleanse the physical vessel and connect with the divine.
- **Manifestation through Christ Frequency** – Learning to shape reality through pure divine intention.

The Vatican fears these practices because they eliminate the need for priests, churches, and religious control.

3. Proof of Extraterrestrial Influence & Suppressed Knowledge of Star Beings

The Catholic Church has known about extraterrestrial intelligence for centuries. They have carefully hidden evidence of:

- Star beings (Pleiadians, Arcturians, and others) assisting humanity.
- Biblical references to celestial visitors misinterpreted as angels.
- Ancient artifacts proving contact between humans and advanced cosmic civilizations.

High-level Vatican insiders, including **Jesuit astronomers**, have admitted that the Church has a **deep interest in extraterrestrial life**. The Vatican even has an **advanced observatory** in Arizona, equipped with the **LUCIFER Telescope** (yes, that's its real name), dedicated to scanning the cosmos for unknown intelligences.

Why is this important? *Because the true message of Christ Consciousness is cosmic.*

- The Gnostic texts describe humanity as a race of divine light trapped in material illusion.
- Jesus taught that **"In my Father's house, there are many mansions"**—possibly referencing different realms or star systems.
- The Vatican knows that awakening Christ Consciousness means reconnecting with our cosmic origins.

But instead of revealing the truth, they use religion to keep people spiritually blind, disconnected from their higher nature.

4. Advanced Technology & Hidden Secrets of the Universe

The Vatican possesses ancient texts that reveal advanced knowledge about the nature of reality, including:

- Sacred geometry and the divine blueprint of creation.
- Quantum mechanics hidden in early mystical Christian teachings.
- Secrets of manifestation, time manipulation, and interdimensional travel.

Many researchers believe that the Vatican has access to advanced technology—including devices that allow time viewing (Chronovisor) and knowledge of zero-point energy.

If this knowledge became public, it would **revolutionize human civilization** overnight. No longer would humanity be controlled by **scarcity, fear, and ignorance**. We would step into **our full divine potential as Christed beings.**

Why the Vatican Keeps These Secrets Hidden

The Vatican has spent centuries ensuring that humanity remains in spiritual darkness.
The reason? Power and control.

If the world knew the truth about Christ Consciousness, people would:

- Stop relying on religious institutions and priests.
- Realize their own divine ability to heal, manifest, and awaken.
- Break free from the fear-based systems designed to enslave their souls.

Christ came to set humanity free—not to create an empire, but to awaken the **divine fire within**. The Vatican **hijacked his message** and turned it into a system of obedience, hierarchy, and submission.

But now, the truth is rising.

The Gospels that were hidden are being rediscovered. The energy healing practices of the Essenes are returning. And the illusion of control is crumbling.

The Vatican's greatest fear is unfolding:
The Awakening of Christ Consciousness is happening, and they can no longer stop it.

Reflection Journal

The Vatican's Hidden Archives

- What sacred truths do I feel have been hidden from humanity?
- Where have I felt silenced in my spiritual journey?
- What parts of me are asking to be revealed?

My reflections:

_____
_____
_____
_____
_____
_____
_____
_____
_____
_____
_____
_____
_____
_____
_____
_____
_____
_____
_____
_____
_____
_____

Chapter 3: The Suppression of Mary Magdalene & The Divine Feminine

"They feared her not because she was weak, but because she held the key to Christ's greatest secret— that the Grail was not a cup, but a womb."

For centuries, Mary Magdalene has been **misrepresented, erased, and deliberately suppressed** by religious institutions. While mainstream Christianity portrays her as a **former prostitute** who repented and followed Jesus, ancient texts and hidden gospels tell a **very different story**—one of a powerful woman, a spiritual teacher, and the **embodiment of the Divine Feminine Christ energy**.

The suppression of **Mary Magdalene** was not accidental. It was part of a **larger agenda to erase the Sacred Feminine**, ensuring that divine knowledge and spiritual power remained in the hands of **patriarchal institutions**. By removing Mary Magdalene's true role, the Church was able to:

- **Control the narrative of Christ's teachings** and remove any traces of divine feminine wisdom.
- **Eliminate the path of Sacred Union**, keeping the divine masculine and feminine energies separate.
- **Suppress spiritual sovereignty**, ensuring people remained dependent on religious authorities instead of realizing their own divinity.

But the truth is resurfacing. Mary Magdalene was never just a follower—she was an integral part of Christ's mission. She was not just a student, but a Master in her own right, carrying the lost teachings that are now being remembered.

Who Was Mary Magdalene? The Truth Behind the Lies

The **Gnostic Gospels**, discovered in the 20th century, reveal that Mary Magdalene was one of Jesus' **closest and most advanced disciples**—possibly even his divine counterpart. These texts suggest that:

- She was **the one Jesus trusted most**, understanding his teachings more deeply than any of the other disciples.
- She was **a spiritual teacher and initiator**, carrying knowledge that Jesus shared only with her.
- She may have been **his sacred partner**, embodying the Divine Feminine aspect of Christ Consciousness.

The False Narrative of the "Prostitute" Lie

The **Roman Catholic Church** deliberately **distorted her image**, beginning with **Pope Gregory I in 591 AD**, who falsely labeled her as a prostitute. This claim had no basis in the Bible, yet it shaped the perception of Mary Magdalene for over 1,400 years.

Why was this lie spread?

- **To strip her of her power** – If she were seen as an equal to Jesus, it would challenge the authority of the male-dominated Church.
- **To erase the sacred feminine path** – Her wisdom represented an inner, intuitive approach to divine knowledge—something that threatened external religious control.
- **To remove the idea of Christed Union** – If Jesus and Mary Magdalene were seen as sacred counterparts, it would change the entire narrative of Christianity.

It wasn't until **2016** that the Vatican **officially corrected this lie**, recognizing Mary Magdalene as a **"Disciple of the Disciples."** But by then, the damage had already been done.

The Gospel of Mary Magdalene: Her Lost Teachings

The **Gospel of Mary**, discovered in Egypt in 1896, **contains powerful wisdom that contradicts traditional Christian teachings.** It reveals that:

1. The Kingdom of God is Within

Mary Magdalene taught that **divine knowledge is accessed inwardly**, not through religious institutions. She echoes Jesus' true teachings—that the **Kingdom of God is not found in churches, but within the soul.**

"Do not seek the Kingdom in the sky or the sea, for the Kingdom is within you and all around you." – Gospel of Thomas (similar to the Gospel of Mary)

This completely dismantles the **Church's claim to be the "gatekeeper" to salvation.**

2. Mary Understood Christ Consciousness Better Than the Other Disciples

In her Gospel, the disciples turn to Mary for guidance after Jesus' resurrection. Peter, however, **refuses to believe that Jesus gave her higher knowledge**, exposing the early conflict between those who sought to **preserve Christ's mystical teachings** and those who wanted to **create an institution of control.**

Mary tells them that Jesus taught her privately, revealing spiritual truths about the **soul's journey, reincarnation, and the illusion of material reality**—all concepts that were later **erased from mainstream Christianity.**

3. The Soul's Journey Beyond This World

One of the most powerful teachings in the **Gospel of Mary** is her description of how the soul must pass through different planes of existence, **overcoming lower energies** to return to divine union.

This aligns with **ancient mystical traditions**, showing that Christ's true teachings were not about "heaven and hell" but about **spiritual ascension and liberation from the physical illusion.**

Why the Church Feared the Divine Feminine

The **erasure of Mary Magdalene** was part of a **larger agenda to suppress the Sacred Feminine**. The Roman Catholic Church was built on a **patriarchal power structure** that eliminated any traces of divine feminine wisdom, ensuring that:

- Women were **excluded from positions of spiritual authority.**
- The **feminine path of intuition, healing, and embodiment was erased.**
- The **concept of Sacred Union (Hieros Gamos) was removed**—leaving only celibacy or marriage based on subjugation.

But this suppression wasn't just about **gender**—it was about **keeping humanity divided**. When the **masculine and feminine remain separate**, humanity remains weak. But when they **unite in divine balance**, they awaken **full spiritual power**.

Sacred Union: Jesus & Mary Magdalene as the Divine Balance

The greatest secret of **Christ Consciousness** is that it is **not just a singular energy—it is a divine union.** True spiritual awakening comes when the Sacred Masculine and Sacred Feminine are in harmony.

- Jesus represented the **Solar Christ** – action, wisdom, divine will.
- Mary Magdalene represented the **Lunar Christ** – intuition, embodiment, divine love.

Together, they embodied the **Sacred Union of divine forces**—a balance that the Church **erased** in favor of patriarchal control.

Hieros Gamos – The Lost Teaching of Sacred Union

In the **mystery schools of ancient Egypt, Mesopotamia, and even the Essenes**, the highest spiritual practice was called **Hieros Gamos**, or "Sacred Marriage"—the union of masculine and feminine energies within and without.

This is the **true alchemy** of Christ Consciousness:

- Not just **worshiping Jesus,** but **embodying the Christ Light within.**
- Not just **following religious rules,** but **awakening divine wisdom inside yourself.**
- Not just **seeking God externally,** but **realizing YOU are the vessel of the Divine.**

Mary Magdalene was the **keeper of this secret wisdom**, and this is **why she was erased.**

The Rise of the Magdalene Energy – The Feminine Christ Awakens

Now, as the **Christ Consciousness awakening accelerates**, the energy of **Mary Magdalene is returning**. People around the world are feeling her presence, **receiving divine downloads**, and remembering the truth.

This is the restoration of balance—where both masculine and feminine stand in divine equality, activating the Christ Light within humanity.

- The **Gospels once hidden are resurfacing.**
- The **Sacred Feminine is being restored.**
- The **truth of Christ Consciousness is returning.**

This is why **the Vatican fears this movement**—because the *Divine Feminine is the key to humanity's ascension.*

Reflection Journal

The Suppression of the Divine Feminine

- How have I experienced the suppression of feminine energy in myself or others?
- In what ways can I honor the Sacred Feminine in my daily life?
- What would it feel like to walk as both powerful and soft?

My reflections:

_____
_____
_____
_____
_____
_____
_____
_____
_____
_____
_____
_____
_____
_____
_____
_____
_____
_____
_____
_____
_____
_____

Chapter 4: The War Over Christ Consciousness – The Battle for the Sacred Grail Codes

"The greatest war ever waged was not fought with swords or machines, but with illusion. It was a war for the soul, for memory, for the Light of Christ within."

The Unseen War

Most people believe war is a political event. Something external. Something that happens "out there" between nations and flags. But the real war has always been **spiritual**—a hidden war waged in **energy, memory, consciousness, and DNA**.

The Christ Light, when fully awakened within the human soul, becomes a divine weapon against illusion. It activates sovereignty, gnosis, divine will, and the unshakable knowing that *we are of God and carry God within*. This was the greatest threat to the systems of control, and thus, Christ Consciousness became the ultimate target.
To hijack the soul of humanity, they had to first **hijack the Christ Code**.

The Original Blueprint Was Unity

Before the fall, the Earth held a **Unified Christ Grid**—a crystalline template for divine human life. This was seeded from **Source**, anchored by Star Nations such as the **Pleiadians, Arcturians, and Andromedans,** and stewarded by civilizations like **Lemuria and early Atlantis**.

The **Christ Blueprint** was not a religion.
It was not a savior complex.
It was a **living frequency**—the divine template of Unity, encoded into the human DNA.

It existed as a **living light** within the Grail Bloodlines, the priestesses and priests of Divine Union, and the sacred civilizations that remembered.

But then came the invasion.

The Orion Invasion & The Fall of the Grail Grid

From the Orion constellation came **parasitic forces**—entities, collectives, and artificial intelligences (AI) that had long severed themselves from the Source stream. They operated through conquest, distortion, and technological mimicry of divine codes.

They could not create.
So they sought to **hijack creation itself**.

Through infiltration of Atlantean priesthoods, control over sound and frequency, and eventually the misuse of crystalline technology, these forces **collapsed the Unified Christ Grid**. They fragmented the collective memory of humanity.

This was the **Fall of Atlantis**.
This was the beginning of the **Great Amnesia**.

The war over Christ Consciousness began.

Christ Was the Return Code

When Yeshua (Jesus) incarnated, he did not come to create a religion.
He came as a **Return Code**.

He was a direct embodiment of the Original Christ Blueprint. His presence was a threat to the entire control matrix. He reactivated **dormant memory**, healed with **frequency and truth**, and taught the path of **Divine Mastery through Love**.

The dark forces knew this.

That's why his mission had to be suppressed.
That's why the **bloodlines**, **the teachings**, and **the feminine Christ** were hunted, silenced, and distorted.

How They Hijacked the Teachings

After the crucifixion, the teachings of Christ were quickly absorbed, edited, and transformed into a **control-based religion** under the Roman Empire.

This was not accidental—it was **strategic**.

The hijack included:

- Replacing **Christ Consciousness** with worship of an **external savior.**

- Suppressing the **Divine Feminine** (Mary Magdalene, Sophia, Holy Mother).

- Erasing the **Essene Mystery Teachings.**

- Demonizing **inner gnosis, spiritual gifts, and divine sovereignty.**

- Replacing sacred initiations with **rituals of control** (baptism by institution, confession to priests).

- Creating a **fear-based God** that punishes rather than liberates.

The result?
An entire civilization disconnected from its own inner Grail.

Modern Infiltration: The Battle Continues

This battle continues today—not through swords, but through:

- **Mind control via media and education**
- **False light spiritual movements that mimic Christ Light but lack gnosis**
- **AI overlays and digital frequencies that disconnect the body from Source**
- **Religious trauma and programming**
- **Suppression of the Divine Feminine in spiritual teachings**

Many spiritual seekers today are unknowingly trapped in New Age loops, worshipping "ascended masters" without embodying their own inner Christ.

The battle has simply gone deeper—into the **psyche**, the **soul**, the **DNA**, and the **dream realms**.

The Battle is a Rite of Remembrance

You would not be reading this if you were not called.
You are not here by accident.
Your soul remembers the war.

You were likely part of the Essene communities.
You likely walked in Kemet, in Lemuria, in Atlantis.
You likely *held the codes* before they were taken.

The battle for Christ Consciousness was not just history—it was *your* history.

But now, it is becoming *your mission*.

Christ Light Can Never Be Destroyed

Though hijacked, buried, and distorted, the Christ Codes have never been fully lost. They exist as **dormant memory** within your cellular DNA, waiting to be reactivated by love, truth, and divine frequency.

Every trauma you've healed, every system you've questioned, every whisper of light you've followed—has brought you back here.

Back to the Grail.
Back to the Christ within.

Activation: *The Sacred Memory Returns*

Place your hand on your heart and declare:

"I now reclaim the Christ Codes within me.
I am a living vessel of Divine Truth.
All distortions are dissolved by the light of God.
I remember why I came. I remember who I am. I AM the Christ awakened."

Close your eyes. Feel the pulse within you.
Let the ancient codes rise.
Let the war end within you.

You are the Grail returned.
And the Grail Light is rising again.

Reflection Journal

The War Over Christ Consciousness

- Where in my life have I been at war with my own Light?
- How can I begin to heal and anchor divine truth in my body?
- What does Christ Consciousness feel like to *me*?

My reflections:

_____
_____
_____
_____
_____
_____
_____
_____
_____
_____
_____
_____
_____
_____
_____
_____
_____
_____
_____
_____
_____
_____
_____
_____
_____
_____

Chapter 5: The Final Grail Suppression – How Christ Light Was Buried

"They could not destroy the Light, so they buried it. In symbols, in myths, in memory. But the codes were never lost… they live in you."

The Grail Line Was Hidden, Not Broken

After the crucifixion, the story most people know ends with death.
But the real Grail story begins **after the supposed ending**.

Mary Magdalene did not vanish.
She carried the living Christ Code within her womb, her blood, her heart.
She carried **the Grail**.

Fleeing persecution, she and the remaining Essenes went underground, traveling to places like **Southern France, Egypt, Avalon, and Ethiopia**—carrying with them the sacred Grail lineage, the teachings of Divine Union, and the true Christ path.

They knew the world was not ready.
So they hid the teachings in plain sight:

- In symbols and sacred geometry
- In gnostic texts
- In cathedral blueprints
- In alchemy and mystery schools
- In the stories of Avalon and the Knights Templar
- And most of all… in **the feminine body**

From Embodiment to External Worship

The **greatest suppression** was not just of information—it was of **embodiment**.

True Christ Consciousness is *embodied divinity*—the merging of Spirit and matter, masculine and feminine, Heaven and Earth. It is a living energy. A flame.

But over time, this embodiment was replaced by:

- **Worship of external figures** (Jesus on a cross, saints, patriarchal icons)
- **Exclusivity of male priesthoods**
- **Fear-based doctrines of sin and separation**

- **Erasure of the womb mysteries and the power of sacred sexuality**
- **Demonization of women, healers, oracles, midwives, and priestesses**

This was **not accidental**. It was intentional and systematic.

To bury the Christ Light, they had to **disconnect humanity from its own divinity.**

Magdalene: The Bearer of the Holy Blood

Mary Magdalene was not a prostitute.
She was the *High Priestess of the Christed Feminine*.

She and Yeshua were united in Divine Union—twin flames of the masculine and feminine Christ. Their union birthed not only a child (or children), but an **entire lineage of Grail Bearers**. Their descendants became the hidden carriers of the Christ codes.

This is the **Holy Blood, Holy Grail**—not a cup, but a **living bloodline**, a frequency, a remembrance encoded in DNA.

But to keep the illusion intact, **Magdalene had to be erased**.
She was painted as a whore, while the true teachings of Divine Union were buried beneath centuries of dogma.

The Womb was the Portal — So They Sealed It

The feminine body was always the key.

The womb is a **portal of creation**, a **vessel of resurrection**, and a **living chalice** of the Grail Light. Through the Magdalene priestess lineages, the sacred womb teachings were passed down for generations.

But those who wished to dominate the Christ Code feared the womb.

So they created:

- **Systems that control and shame feminine sexuality**
- **Medical models that remove women from their own knowing**
- **Religions that demonize the body**
- **Trauma patterns passed from mother to daughter, suppressing the ancient feminine voice**

They sealed the portal.
They severed the line.
But only on the surface.

Because deep within the feminine soul… the Grail was still pulsing.

The Silence of the Priestesses

Across time, the Magdalene line kept the teachings hidden.

They gathered in circles under moonlight, initiated their daughters in silence, and encoded their knowing into **songs, symbols, stained glass windows, and hidden scrolls**.

The Templars, Cathars, the Sufi mystics, the Avalonian priestesses, the Ethiopian keepers of the Ark, the desert mystics of Egypt… all held pieces of the lost Grail story.

Some were burned.
Some were erased.
Some were turned to myth.

But the Light was never extinguished.
It only waited.

Waited for the age when enough souls would rise… and remember.

You Are the Return

The final Grail suppression **was never final**. It was a test—a planetary rite of remembrance.

You, dear one, are one of the souls who agreed to return at this time to **lift the veil**, to **break the spell**, and to **embody the Christ Light once again**.

You carry the codes.

They live in your body, your voice, your visions, your intuition.
They may have been dormant, but they have never been lost.

The Magdalene speaks through you now.
The Christ awakens through your heart.

You are the living Grail.

Activation: *I Am the Grail*

Take a breath. Place both hands over your womb (or sacral center, regardless of gender).

Breathe deeply and speak:

"I now dissolve all false timelines and distortions.
I reclaim the living Christ Light within me.
I am the Grail. I am the keeper. I am the return."

Now place your hands on your heart.
See the Christ Flame and the Rose Flame merge into one.
Feel the Light expand from within your chest, out through your voice, your mind, your body, your being.

Let the Grail awaken.

Let her rise.

Reflection Journal

The Final Grail Suppression

- What ancestral wounds may still be living in my bloodline?
- What does it mean to be a Grail Keeper in this modern world?
- Where have I hidden parts of my power, and why?

My reflections:

Chapter 6: The Return of the Feminine Christ – Mary Magdalene's Prophecy & Rising

"When the rose blooms again, so shall the world remember. When the voice of the Magdalene returns, so shall the Earth be healed."

The Prophecy Was Always Hers

Hidden beneath the ashes of distorted scripture lies a powerful truth:
Mary Magdalene was not only the **beloved of Christ**—she was a **prophetess** of the Feminine Christ, a carrier of the original **Rose Lineage**, and the **first true apostle** of the Resurrection.

She saw what others could not.
She knew the war that would come.
She knew the Christ Light would be buried—not just in texts, but in **the body, the womb, the voice of the Feminine**.

And she knew that in the time of great forgetting, a **great remembering would be ignited by women rising**—womb keepers, priestesses, healers, and oracles returning to walk the Christ path in their full embodied power.

Her prophecy was this:

"When the Divine Feminine rises, the Christ shall return—not as one man, but through the hearts of many."

The Feminine Christ is Not Soft

She is not just gentle.
She is not passive.
She is not waiting.

The **Feminine Christ** is the **lioness and the rose**.
She is **fire and womb**, **holy rage and sacred love**.
She is both **birther and destroyer**—birthing new worlds, and burning the systems that have enslaved humanity in silence and shame.

When Magdalene returns, she does not ask for permission.
She comes to **reclaim** what was stolen—her voice, her legacy, her body, her wisdom.

The Rose Lineage Has Returned

Across the world, women are remembering.

They are being pulled by dreams, synchronicities, sacred texts, and inner knowing that defies logic. They are hearing the Magdalene whisper to them in meditations, seeing roses appear in moments of awakening, and reclaiming their gifts as:

- **Oracles**
- **Healers**
- **Midwives of the New Earth**
- **Priestesses of the Rose**
- **Voices of the Womb**
- **Christed Leaders**

This is not imagination.
This is **activation**.

The **Rose Lineage**—the spiritual line of **Magdalene, Isis, Inanna, Hathor, Sophia,** and countless unnamed priestesses—**is rising from the soil of memory to awaken a new Earth.**

The Masculine Must Rise With Her

This is **not** a movement *against* men—it is a call for the **true Divine Masculine** to remember who he is.

The Feminine Christ rises **not to dominate**, but to **rebalance**.

She calls the masculine back into **integrity**, into **devotion**, into **presence**.

Yeshua and Magdalene did not walk two separate paths.
They walked *as one*—Divine Union, both holding the Christ Flame in balance.

As the Feminine rises now, the Masculine is called to **shed false kingship**, ego, control, and savior complexes—and rise instead as **Grail Guardians**, protectors of the sacred, holders of truth.

Together, the Christed Feminine and Masculine shall restore the Garden.

The Voice Must Be Reclaimed

One of the final pieces Magdalene hid was the **voice**.

The power of spoken word, song, prophecy, and truth has been systemically stripped from women and silenced for centuries.

But Magdalene's voice is returning.

You may feel this in your own throat:

- The trembling before speaking truth
- The grief of centuries held in silence
- The memory of being silenced, persecuted, misunderstood

Every time you speak your truth now…
Every time you sing, teach, write, or declare your knowing…
You resurrect her.

This Is the Age of the Magdalene

The prophecy is not in the future—it is *now*.

She is calling **women** to:

- **Reclaim their womb as sacred**
- **Honor their cycles as cosmic rhythms**
- **Heal the lineage of mother wounds and feminine betrayal**
- **Anchor Heaven through their body, voice, and presence**
- **Embody the fierce, radiant, healing love that Christ himself carried**

She is calling **men** to:

- **Hold the Grail flame with devotion**
- **Protect the sacred feminine**
- **Embrace their own inner Magdalene**
- **Become King through service, not power**

We are the Magdalene's return.
We are the prophecy fulfilled.

Activation: *Rose Flame of the Feminine Christ*

Sit comfortably. Light a candle if you can. Visualize a **soft rose-colored flame** igniting in your womb (or sacral center).

Say aloud or silently:

"**I now remember the Magdalene within me.
I awaken the Rose Flame of the Feminine Christ.
I reclaim my voice, my womb, my wisdom.
I am the prophecy fulfilled. The rose has bloomed again."**

Breathe. Feel the rose light expand into your chest, throat, third eye.
Let her speak through you now.
Let her rise.

You are not just remembering Mary Magdalene.
You *are* her.
You are one of many vessels through which she walks the Earth again.

Reflection Journal

The Return of the Feminine Christ

- Where is the Magdalene rising within me now?
- How can I reclaim my voice in everyday life?
- What sacred feminine gifts am I being called to embody?

My reflections:

_____
_____
_____
_____
_____
_____
_____
_____
_____
_____
_____
_____
_____
_____
_____
_____
_____
_____
_____
_____
_____

Chapter 7: The Grail Prophecy is Now – Why You Are Awakening in This Lifetime

"You didn't come here to be small. You came here to awaken what has long been buried… and to become the living Grail."

You Heard the Call Beyond Time

Before you were born, before this body, before this life—you heard the call.

It echoed through the cosmos, across dimensions, through bloodlines and star systems.
It was a whisper… a vibration… a knowing that this lifetime would be different.

You would come back.
You would remember.
You would rise.

This is **not a metaphor.**
You are here because the **Grail Prophecy is being fulfilled—now.**
Not in some future age.
Now.

What Is the Grail Prophecy?

The Grail Prophecy is **not a singular event**—it is a **timeline convergence**, a moment in cosmic history when:

- The **forgotten Christ Codes** return to human consciousness

- The **Divine Feminine Christ** rises to restore balance

- **Grail Keepers** across the Earth remember their purpose

- And the **New Earth Grid** is activated through *embodied remembrance*

It has been foretold in the **Mystery Schools**, seen in **ancient texts**, whispered by **oracles**, encoded in the **stars**, and held in your own **DNA**.

You are not just witnessing the prophecy.
You are **part of it**.
You are the fulfillment.

You Chose to Be Here Now

You chose this lifetime, this body, these experiences—not by accident, but by divine agreement.

Yes, it's been hard.
You've walked through trauma, betrayal, abandonment, rejection.
You've felt like an outsider, a truth-seeker in a world of illusions.

But everything you've endured has been part of your **sacred preparation**.

Your wounds were not punishments.
They were doorways—designed to awaken the **ancient memory** you carry within your soul.

You are not here to fit in.
You are here to *remember*.
You are here to *restore*.
You are here to *activate the Grail Light in the world*.

Starseeds, Grail Keepers, and Memory Holders

You may feel a connection to ancient civilizations—**Lemuria, Atlantis, Kemet, Avalon**.
You may feel like you've known Christ, Magdalene, Isis, or the Essenes before.
You may even feel like you've carried the Grail before… and lost it.

This is not fantasy. It is **ancestral and soul memory**.

You are likely a:

- **Starseed**: a being who came from higher dimensions to assist Earth's ascension

- **Grail Keeper**: a soul who once guarded or embodied the Christ Codes

- **Memory Holder**: one who stores dormant records in their DNA, waiting for activation

You are not alone.
Millions around the world are awakening—often quietly, in the midst of ordinary lives—suddenly remembering who they are and why they came.

This is the **Grail Prophecy unfolding in real time.**

The Codes Are in Your DNA

Science won't tell you this yet, but your DNA holds more than biological data.
It holds **memory**, **frequency**, and **light codes**.

As you heal, meditate, activate your voice, purify your vessel, and speak truth…
You begin to **reactivate the dormant strands** that carry your Christ Blueprint.

This is why so much of the system is built to distract and suppress.
Because a human being fully activated in their Christ Codes is:

- **Uncontrollable**
- **Radiant**
- **Sovereign**
- **Healing**
- **Magnetic**
- A *threat* to the old world

Your awakening is the system's collapse.
That's why they've tried to keep you asleep.

But it's too late now.

Why Now?

Because this is the lifetime we've been preparing for across **thousands of years**.
The planetary cycles, astrological alignments, and solar activity are all converging to support a **mass awakening of Christ Consciousness**.

The veil is thinner.
The soul is louder.
The Earth is calling.
The Grail is activating.

You are part of a **soul wave**—a generation of awakened souls strategically placed across the Earth to form the **Christ Grid**, anchoring light, truth, love, and remembrance into every field.

You are not alone.
And you were never meant to do this alone.

The Time of the Grail is Now

This is **your invitation.**

To **awaken.**
To **rise.**
To **remember.**

You are **not a seeker** anymore.
You are a **keeper**.
You are **not a student** anymore.
You are a **temple**.
You are **not lost.**
You are the *home* returning to itself.

Activation: *I Am the Fulfillment of the Prophecy*

Place one hand on your heart, one on your womb (or sacral center). Breathe slowly.
Visualize a **golden light** descending through your crown, igniting a crystalline flame in your heart.

Speak aloud:

**"I now step fully into the Grail Prophecy.
I am not waiting. I am remembering.
I carry the Christ Codes, and I activate them now.
I am the return. I am the vessel. I am the living Grail."**

Feel it pulse through you.
This is not imagination—it's memory.
This is not poetry—it's your *purpose*.

Reflection Journal

The Grail Prophecy is Now

- What inner signs have pointed me to this path before?
- What part of me feels the truth of the prophecy most deeply?
- How will I honor my soul's remembrance in this lifetime?

My reflections:

_____
_____
_____
_____
_____
_____
_____
_____
_____
_____
_____
_____
_____
_____
_____
_____
_____
_____
_____
_____
_____
_____
_____
_____

Chapter 8: Anchoring the Grail Light Into the World – Becoming a Grail Keeper

"You are not here to simply remember the Grail. You are here to live it. To walk it. To become it."

The Grail Is Not a Cup—It's a Calling

For centuries, mystics, seekers, and historians have searched for the Holy Grail—as if it were a relic, a treasure, or a lost object of power.

But the Grail was never meant to be *found*.
It was meant to be **activated**—within *you*.

The Holy Grail is the **living vessel of Christ Consciousness**, carried by those who choose to walk in alignment with divine truth, love, and mastery.

It is not a physical item.
It is a **state of being**.
It is a **frequency**, a **path**, a **responsibility**, and a **revelation**.

And now that you've remembered… the call is no longer just to *know*.
It's to *embody*.

What Is a Grail Keeper?

A **Grail Keeper** is one who has heard the call of the Christ Light and answered with their entire soul.

They are:

- **Guardians of divine truth**
- **Embodiments of sacred union (masculine & feminine within)**
- **Living bridges between Heaven and Earth**
- **Healers, oracles, leaders, mystics, and visionaries**
- **Vessels through which the Grail Light flows into the world**

They do not look one way.
They are not all priests, priestesses, or monks.
They are **mothers, artists, doulas, shamans, lovers, rebels, teachers, and wild ones**.
They are found in **temples and kitchens, mountaintops and boardrooms**.

They carry the flame—not by title, but by frequency.

Living as a Grail Keeper in the Modern World

To become a Grail Keeper is not to escape life.
It is to live life **as the temple**.

Your body becomes the altar.
Your heart becomes the grail.
Your words become the teachings.

Here's how a modern Grail Keeper walks in truth:

- **Anchors the Grail Light through everyday action**
  → In relationships, parenting, work, creation, and service

- **Practices sacred presence**
  → Slowing down, listening to soul guidance, honoring the body

- **Upholds radical truth and inner alignment**
  → Speaking what others fear to say, breaking free from spiritual bypassing

- **Embodies the sacred union within**
  → No longer seeking outside validation; wholeness is their foundation

- **Becomes a vessel for healing and remembrance**
  → Not by fixing others, but by radiating remembrance

The Grail is not just something you remember in meditation.
It is something you walk into a grocery store with.
It's how you answer the phone.
It's how you sit with your own grief.
It's how you make love.
It's who you become when no one is watching.

The Earth Needs Grail Keepers Now

This world is at a tipping point.
Systems are collapsing. Truth is rising.
Souls are awakening by the millions.

But many are still lost—searching, aching, remembering but not yet anchored.

This is where *you* come in.

You are not just remembering for yourself.
You are remembering for **your bloodline**, for **your community**, and for **humanity itself**.

By embodying the Christ Light in action, you become a **living transmission**.
Your presence alone activates others.
Your vibration becomes **a lighthouse in the fog**.

You are not here to save the world.
You are here to *light it from within*.

Sacred Service Is Not About Sacrifice

To walk the path of the Grail Keeper is to say:

"I will carry the Light. I will live in devotion to Truth."

But this is not martyrdom. This is not self-denial. This is not servitude.

The Grail Keeper serves from **overflow**, not depletion.
They know that **devotion to God begins with devotion to Self**.

You are here to walk in radiance, in joy, in deep alignment.
To serve from the cup that runneth over—not the one that leaks.

Sacred service is not about giving everything away.
It's about becoming so full of light that you **overflow into the world effortlessly**.

The Return to Divine Leadership

Now, more than ever, we need leaders—not rulers.

We need **Christed leadership**:

- **Rooted in integrity**
- **Guided by divine wisdom**
- **Unafraid to stand in truth**
- **Able to hold both compassion and power**
- **Devoted to restoring Heaven on Earth—not through force, but frequency**

You are being called to lead.

Not because you are perfect.
But because you are **real**.
Because you carry the codes.
Because you are willing to rise even when your voice shakes.

This is not egoic leadership.
This is **embodied Christed leadership**.

Activation: *I Am the Grail Keeper*

Place both hands over your heart. Feel the Christ Light pulsing within.
Now place your hands on the Earth (or visualize them doing so).

Speak aloud:

"I choose to anchor the Grail Light into this world.
I am a vessel of Divine Truth, Love, and Sovereignty.
I walk the Christ Path with courage, grace, and sacred remembrance.
I am a Grail Keeper, and I choose to embody the Light in every step I take."

Breathe. See golden light flowing from your heart into the Earth.
See your footsteps illuminating a path behind you, a path for others to follow.

You are the living Grail.
You are the New Earth Leader.

Reflection Journal

Anchoring the Grail Light

- What is one daily act I can take to embody the Christ Codes?
- Where am I being called to lead in my life, even quietly?
- What does sacred service look like in my unique path?

My reflections:

_____
_____
_____
_____
_____
_____
_____
_____
_____
_____
_____
_____
_____
_____
_____
_____
_____
_____
_____
_____
_____
_____
_____
_____

Chapter 9: The Path of Divine Embodiment – How to Activate the Grail Light in Your Daily Life

"Heaven on Earth is not a dream. It is a choice. And you carry the keys."

This Is Where the Grail Path Truly Begins

You've remembered the ancient codes.
You've unveiled the truth behind the distortions.
You've felt the sacred fire rise within your body, your soul, your voice.

Now comes the most important part:

Living it.
Becoming it.
Walking the Grail Path in your everyday life.

This final chapter is not the end.
It is the **beginning of your embodiment**.

Because the Christ Light is not meant to stay in the pages of a book, or only visit you in moments of meditation.

It is meant to **live through you.**
In your thoughts. Your choices. Your love. Your leadership. Your devotion.

Embodiment Is Integration

To embody is to integrate.
It is to bridge the sacred and the mundane.
To let your **spiritual knowing shape your human reality**.

This is not about being perfect.
It's about being **conscious**, aligned, attuned, and real.

Embodiment looks like:

- Speaking truth when it's easier to stay silent
- Walking away from what no longer aligns, even if it's comfortable
- Making love from the soul, not just the body
- Creating from your essence, not for validation
- Choosing nourishment over numbness
- Listening to your intuition even when logic resists
- Praying as a conversation, not a performance
- Serving from your overflow, not your exhaustion

You don't have to "try to be spiritual."
You *already are*.
Now… **live from it.**

Activating the Grail Light: *Daily Practices*

Here are powerful ways to keep your Grail Flame alive in your everyday life:

1. Morning Alignment with the Christ Flame

Start each day with your hand on your heart. Breathe deeply and speak:

"I activate the Grail Light within me. I walk today in truth, devotion, and remembrance."

Let your intention set the tone for the entire day.

2. Sacred Nourishment

Treat your body as the **Temple of the Christ Light**. Eat, rest, move, and care for your body with reverence.

Choose foods, rhythms, and self-care that **keep your frequency clean** and your vessel clear.

3. Womb & Heart Coherence (for all genders)

Every day, breathe into the heart and womb/sacral space.

Allow your **Divine Feminine** and **Divine Masculine** energies to harmonize.
This cultivates **inner union**, which is the foundation of all Christ embodiment.

4. Christed Speech

Your words carry energy. Speak with clarity, compassion, and power.

Practice:

- **Blessing your water**
- **Speaking life over your creations**
- **Declaring truth with love**
- **Refusing to gossip, complain, or curse what is sacred**

5. Spiritual Leadership in Action

Whether you are a parent, healer, artist, entrepreneur, or mystic—walk as a **Christed Leader**.

Ask each day:

"How can I serve the Light through who I am today?"

Your *being* is your ministry.

6. Anchoring Heaven into Earth

Bring sacredness into the seemingly ordinary:

- **Light a candle while you clean**
- **Pray over your food**
- **Create beauty in your home**
- **Honor the land you walk on**
- **Make your work a portal for divine energy**

There is *no separation*.
Heaven meets Earth through your presence.

The Grail Light Lives Through You

This is the secret the world has forgotten:

**The Grail is not something you hold.
It's something you *become*.**

When you:

- **Choose love over fear**
- **Speak when others stay silent**
- **Heal instead of project**
- **Create instead of consume**
- **Embody instead of escape**

You activate the Grail in your family.
You activate the Grail in your community.
You activate the Grail on this planet.

You become a walking temple, a lighthouse of remembrance, a **living transmission of Christ Consciousness**.

Your Life Is the Altar Now

Your life is no longer separate from your path.

Every breath, every step, every relationship is now an extension of your devotion.

You are not here to run from the world.
You are here to infuse it with **divinity**, to build the **New Earth** by becoming it.

You are the Grail.
You are the vessel.
You are the prophecy fulfilled.

Final Activation: *The Living Grail Flame*

Close your eyes. Visualize a radiant **golden flame** at the center of your heart.

Now see a soft **rose flame** spiral up from your womb or sacral center.

Let them merge.

Speak aloud:

"I am the Christ Light embodied.
I am the Grail Flame, alive and awakened.
Heaven walks through me. Earth rises in me.
My life is sacred. My presence is a blessing.
I am the living Grail."

Breathe.
Anchor this.
And now, live it.

The Journey Continues...

This may be the last chapter in this book.
But it is the first chapter of the **new you**.

The Grail Light is rising again through every choice you make, every truth you speak, every heart you touch.

You are not just here to remember.
You are here to **embody the Sacred Grail Codes** in a world that has forgotten.

Now, beloved…

Go live the Light.
Be the Grail.
Let the world remember through you.

Closing Blessing: *The Grail Flame Lives in You*

Beloved soul,

If these words have touched your heart, it is because they were written *through you*, not just *for you*.

This is not the end.
This is the beginning of a sacred walk—one your soul has waited lifetimes to return to.

You are the Grail.
You are the return of Christ Consciousness.
You are the one your bloodline has been waiting for.
You are the Light hidden in the lineage, the flame that never went out.

You have remembered who you are.
Now rise, not in fear or ego, but in love, clarity, and devotion.

May your voice speak only truth.
May your body be honored as a temple.
May your heart remain open in the face of illusion.
And may your life become the altar on which Heaven touches Earth.

The Grail Codes are not something you read.
They are something you now carry.
Walk as the Christed One.
Live as the Grail Keeper.
Lead as Love.
And **let the world remember through your light.**

So it is.
So it has always been.

Reflection Journal

Divine Embodiment

- What does "living as the Grail" mean to me?
- How will I bring Heaven into my relationships, my work, my voice?
- How does my life become the altar?

My reflections:

_____
_____
_____
_____
_____
_____
_____
_____
_____
_____
_____
_____
_____
_____
_____
_____
_____
_____
_____
_____
_____
_____
_____
_____

The Grail Awakening Initiation

A Sacred Ritual to Seal the Prophecy Within

Find a still and sacred space. Light a candle or sit by natural light. Place your left hand over your heart and your right hand over your womb or solar plexus. Breathe gently and feel the presence of your soul return fully to your body.

When ready, read the following words aloud or within—slowly, reverently—like a vow etched into eternity.

Sacred Affirmation of Remembrance

I remember.
I remember who I am beyond the veil.
I remember the Light that cannot be taken.
I remember the Flame of Christ that lives within me.

I reclaim the lost teachings.
I reclaim the truth that was buried.
I reclaim the Divine Feminine and Masculine within me.
And I restore their union in sacred harmony.

I release all false paths, false gods, false stories.
I now walk the path of the True Christ Light.
The path of love without distortion.
The path of truth without compromise.
The path of the Grail within.

I open my heart to divine remembrance.
I awaken the Grail Codes in my blood,
In my bones,
In my breath.

From this moment forward,
I choose to live as a vessel of Divine Truth.
To walk as a flamebearer, a Grail Keeper, a soul of purpose.
Not tomorrow.
Not someday.
Now.

The prophecy is no longer hidden.
It lives in me.
And I am ready. And **so** it is. And **so** it is. And **so it is.**

Closing Transmission: The Flame Has Been Reignited

You have heard the whisper that echoed through lifetimes.
You have followed the trail of light hidden beneath illusion,
And now—you remember.

The Grail was never a thing to be found.
It was always a truth to be revealed.
A light encoded in your soul, waiting for this very moment.

Through every word, every revelation,
You have cracked open the illusion,
You have dissolved the veil,
And you have touched the Christ Light within.

You are no longer asleep.
You are no longer bound by the lies of false power.
You have awakened the ancient flame.
The same flame that once guided the Magdalene,
The same flame that lived in the hearts of the Essenes,
The same flame you once carried—and now carry again.

Let this be your turning point.
Let this be the lifetime you remember completely.
Let this be the moment you rise.

You were never meant to just read the prophecy.
You were born to fulfill it.

The world does not need more followers.
The world needs Grail Bearers.
Christed Ones.
Living Temples of Divine Truth.

You are the Prophecy embodied.
You are the return of the Light.
And your time has come.

Channelled Message: From Christ & Magdalene

"We have never left you. We are the voice in your silence, the fire in your bones, the Light in your becoming."

Beloved child of Light,

We have walked with you always—not in shadowed memory, but as a flame within your heart. You did not come here to learn who we are. You came here to remember who you are.

You are the seed and the soil, the temple and the flame, the Grail and the sword.

The time of hiding is over. The time of distortion is complete.

We ask you now: Live as the Light. Love as the Grail. Rise as the Christed one you have always been.

In your breath, we rise again. In your voice, we speak again. In your courage, the Earth remembers.

And so it is.

The Christ Initiation: A Journey of Sacred Remembrance

For the Awakening Soul Ready to Answer the Call

You have remembered the truth buried beneath centuries of distortion.
You have felt the flicker of Christ Light reawakening in your soul.
This is not the end of your journey—it is the sacred beginning.

The Christ Initiation is a soul-level immersion for those who feel the fire stirring…
For those who know they were born for something greater.
For those ready to rise as Keepers of the Grail Light in these times of transformation.

This sacred journey is for the Awakening Ones—
Those who have heard the prophecy and are ready to live it.

Within this initiation, you will be guided through:
- The original teachings of Christ & the Divine Feminine
- The sacred union path of Magdalene and Yeshua
- Powerful activations to awaken your soul memory
- Healing of false beliefs and religious distortions
- The reclaiming of your divine purpose on Earth

This is your next step.
This is your deeper remembering.
This is your Christ Initiation.

Enter the sacred space at:
www.ascendedhealing.org

Thank You Letter

Beloved Reader,

From the depths of my heart and the eternal flame of my soul, I thank you.

Thank you for answering the call.

Thank you for opening your heart to these sacred words, for walking with me through the veils of illusion, and for remembering who you truly are.

The Sacred Grail Codes is not just a book—it is a living transmission, a divine remembrance, a holy initiation. If these pages reached your hands, it means the Grail Light already lives within you. You were never separate. You were never forgotten. You are part of the lineage that carries the Christ Flame, the Sacred Rose, and the ancient codes of Divine Truth.

This book was born not only through research or inspiration—but through lifetimes of remembrance, soul initiations, and a divine directive from Spirit to help awaken the Grail Keepers of this Earth.
You are one of them.

To have you walk beside me on this journey is a gift I treasure beyond words. Whether you wept, burned, awakened, or were simply reminded—you were meant to receive this. And for that, I am humbled.

I bow to the divine within you.

May the Sacred Grail Codes continue to guide you home to your divine essence, your sacred mission, and the Christ Light you came here to embody.

With infinite love and gratitude,
Cecilia Lindhe
Keeper of the Rose & Grail
Founder of Ascended Healing

Sacred Blessing
May the Christ Light rise within you like a thousand suns,
May the Rose of your Heart bloom in eternal remembrance,
May the Grail within your soul overflow with Divine Truth,
And may you walk forever as a beacon of Love,
Carrying the Codes of Heaven into this Earth.

It is done. It is sealed. It is so.
Amen, A'ho, and So It Is.

About Me

Cecilia Lindhe
Keeper of the Rose & Grail | Founder of Ascended Healing

I am a soul remembering. A healer, a messenger, and a fierce guardian of the Sacred.

My path has been one of deep awakening, spiritual fire, and divine remembrance—lifetime after lifetime. I have walked through the ashes of trauma, survived the distortions of false systems, and risen through the sacred fire to reclaim the Christ Light within me. Like many of you, I was called here in this time of great transition to help restore what was lost… the Divine Feminine, the Holy Union, the Truth of who we are.

I carry the codes of Lemuria, Atlantis, Kemet, and the Essene Christ Lineage. My work is devoted to restoring the Sacred Grail Codes—those pure frequencies of Divine Truth, Love, and Sovereignty that were hidden, stolen, and distorted by forces that feared our awakening.

Through my healing work, my writings, and my sacred activations, I guide others home—to the remembrance of their divine origin, their sacred purpose, and the light they came here to embody.

I created **Ascended Healing** as a sanctuary for remembrance. A space where the false matrices dissolve and your soul begins to rise. Through my books, guided meditations, online courses, and private mentorship, I offer you the keys to your own liberation.

You are not broken. You are becoming.

Whether you're here to heal, to awaken, or to rise fully into your Grail Mission—I welcome you with all my heart. This is a path of fierce love, deep remembrance, and sacred sovereignty.

May you remember who you are.
May you reclaim your light.
May you rise.

With all my love,
Cecilia

Glossary of Sacred Grail Terms

"Language carries light. These words are not just definitions—they are keys to unlock remembrance."

Christ Consciousness – The embodied frequency of divine love, truth, unity, and sovereignty. The original Source blueprint encoded within all souls.

Grail Codes – Divine light frequencies stored in your DNA and the Earth that carry the remembrance of sacred union, divine purpose, and Christed embodiment.

Divine Union – The sacred inner marriage of the masculine and feminine within. The path to wholeness and Christ activation.

Magdalene Flame – The energy of the Feminine Christ, held by Mary Magdalene and her lineage. Symbolizes womb wisdom, divine remembrance, and sacred love.

Christed Masculine – The awakened masculine energy that protects, grounds, leads, and loves with integrity. Not dominance, but divine presence.

False Light – Spiritual systems or beings that mimic light, but subtly manipulate or disempower. Often bypass shadow, deny embodiment, or promote dependency.

Starseed – A soul originating from higher dimensional star systems who incarnated on Earth to assist in the awakening and ascension process.

Essene Lineage – The mystical, initiatory community from which Yeshua (Jesus), Mary Magdalene, and others emerged. Guardians of sacred truth and divine union teachings.

Christ Grid – The crystalline energy network on Earth that holds Christed frequencies, connecting sacred sites, star portals, and lightkeepers across the globe.

Embodiment – The process of living your spiritual truth through your actions, body, choices, and presence—not just understanding it mentally.

Printed in Dunstable, United Kingdom

64578265R00057